What to Expect When You're Expecting Hatchlings:

A GUIDE FOR CROCODILIAN PARENTS
(and Curious Kids)

Bridget Heos

ILLUSTRATED BY Stéphane Jorisch

M MILLBROOK PRESS · MINNEAPOLIS

**For my three hatchlings,
Johnny, Richie, and J.J.
—B.H.**

The author wishes to thank John Brueggen, director, St. Augustine Alligator Farm
Zoological Park, St. Augustine, Florida, for sharing his expertise.

Text copyright © 2012 by Bridget Heos
Illustrations copyright © 2012 by Stéphane Jorisch

Millbrook Press
A division of Lerner Publishing Group, Inc.
241 First Avenue North
Minneapolis, MN 55401 U.S.A.

Website address: www.lernerbooks.com

Main body text set in Imperfect 13/18.
Typeface provided by T.26 Digital Type Foundry.

Library of Congress Cataloging-in-Publication Data

Heos, Bridget.
    What to expect when you're expecting hatchlings : a guide for crocodilian
parents (and curious kids) / by Bridget Heos ; illustrated by Stéphane Jorisch.
        p.   cm. — (Expecting animal babies)
    ISBN 978—0—7613—5860—2 (lib. bdg. : alk. paper)
    1. Crocodylidae—Infancy—Juvenile literature. I. Jorisch, Stéphane, ill. II. Title.
QL666.C925H46 2012
597.98'1392—dc23   2011022232

Manufactured in the United States of America
1 − BC − 12/31/11

CONGRATULATIONS, crocodilian parents-to-be!

You have little ones on the way. You must be thrilled! You're probably nervous too. Parenting is a big job. Luckily, you're very protective, aren't you, tough guy . . . and gal!

Mamas, you will do most of the parenting. But some of you guys, such as muggers and Nile crocodiles, are hands-on—or should I say claws-on?—daddies.

No matter what kind of crocodilian you are, don't worry. You have instincts. These will tell you how to be a mama or a daddy. If you're still curious, read on. Whether you're an alligator, a caiman, a crocodile, or even a funny-looking gharial, you'll find answers to all your questions here. But there's one condition: don't eat the book!

Q. okay, first things first.
Just how big and tough will my babies be?

A. Um . . . sorry. They'll be the opposite. I won't say they'll be wimps (because you might eat me). Let's say they'll be helpless while they're so little. Luckily, you crocodilians are good parents.

4

Q. Excuse me. I'm an alligator.
I prefer not to be called crocodilian.

A. Actually, alligators are crocodilians. Alligators, crocodiles, caimans, and gharials are all members of the crocodilian family. Caimans are closely related to alligators, but they tend to be smaller. Gharials have long, narrow snouts. I apologize for lumping you all together, but you are, in fact, in the same family.

As I was saying, your babies are tiny when they first hatch. You'll need to protect your youngsters from raccoons, wildcats, and more. To them, your hatchlings are fun-sized snacks!

Rest assured that your babies will grow fast. Then how the tables will turn! Not so tough, now, are you, Mr. Raccoon? Chomp! Chomp!

But we're getting way ahead of ourselves. You haven't even laid your eggs yet!

Q. That's right!
Where should I lay my eggs?

A. Find some land next to the water where you swim. American crocodiles and Australian saltwater crocs, you like salty water. However, your hatchlings can only handle sort of salty water. Lay the eggs next to a mangrove swamp, a lagoon, a tidal marsh, or an estuary. Those are places where freshwater and seawater mix. (It's also where lots of yummy animals hang out!)

You other crocodilians swim mostly in freshwater. Remember: *fresh* doesn't mean clean. Don't lay your eggs next to a fancy swimming pool! *Freshwater* simply means it doesn't have salt. It can have mud and bugs. The more, the better! If you like freshwater, lay your eggs next to a swamp, a pond, a lake, a river, a bayou, or a freshwater marsh.

Make sure the spot you choose is high enough that it won't flood. If your eggs get covered in water, your babies might drown before they hatch! Now build your nest.

Q. A nest? In a tree?

A. No! You're not a bird! And anyway, your nest is too big for a tree. It should be about 3 feet (0.9 meters) high and 8 feet (2.4 m) across. Make it with leaves, grass, and muck. You don't need to sit on the eggs to warm them. As the plants rot, they'll keep the eggs warm and toasty.

Not all crocodilians build nests. Some of you, including gharials, dig a sandy hole instead. It may not be as fancy as a nest, but it works just as well. The sun heats the sand, which keeps the eggs warm.

As you build your nest, your eggs are growing inside your body. Be sure to follow a strict diet. When you eat a cow or a monkey or a hippo, don't be dainty. Swallow the meat and the bones. Bones give you calcium, which makes your babies' shells nice and hard.

Soon your nest will be complete. Then . . . ta-da! You'll lay a clutch (or group) of sturdy eggs.

Q. What do I do after I lay the eggs?

A. You stand guard! Many animals steal eggs to eat as treats. Don't let them! Dig a wallow—a muddy area that fills with water—next to the nest. Now, lie very still. If a monitor lizard, a stork, or a wild pig comes along, scare it away by hissing and roaring. Or just eat it!

Don't feel bad. It's a predator—an animal that hunts and eats other animals. And predators are terrible. Oops, I forgot that you crocodilians are also predators. Never mind!

Nile crocodile daddies, you sometimes help guard the nest. But you may need to hunt at the same time that Mama is chasing away a predator. While this is happening, another animal may steal your eggs.

Q. What happens inside the shells?

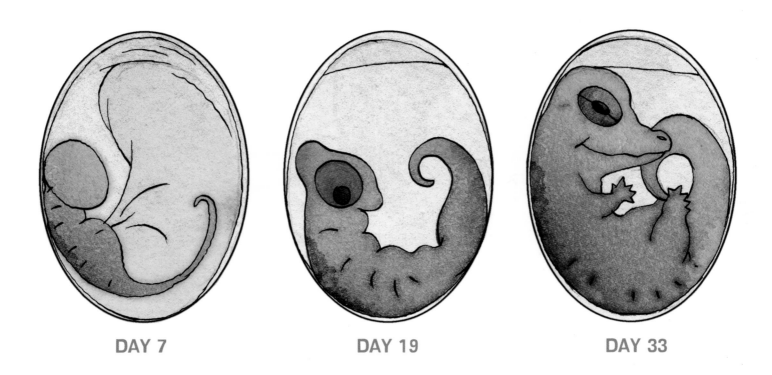

DAY 7   DAY 19   DAY 33

A. Your babies grow. At first, they have big eyes and curled-up tails. To tell the truth, they look a little like sea horses! But thanks to the yummy egg yolk in there, they'll keep growing. Soon they begin to look like itty-bitty alligators or crocodiles.

Whether your babies become boys or girls depends on the temperature in the nest. For many species, if your eggs are very warm, your hatchlings will be males. If they're cooler, they'll be females. This is why girl crocodilians say, "Girls are cool. Boys drool." And boys say, "Boys are hot. Girls are not."

DAY 56

Average temperatures mean some males and some females. Also, the temperature might not be the same in all parts of your nest. In that case, you'll have a mix of boys and girls.

Q. How will I know when my eggs
are ready to hatch?

A. Two or three months after laying the eggs, you'll get a warm feeling in your heart. Actually, it will be more like a loud ringing in your ears. Your babies will make a funny sound from inside their shells. It's like a duck barking or a dog quacking. We'll call it a quark. When one quarks, they all quark.

The hatchlings are saying, "It's crowded in here. I have a leg cramp."

"When do I eat my first water buffalo?"

"Which way to the beach?"

Actually, no one knows what they're saying because nobody speaks hatchling. But for you, these noises mean, "It's go time!"

First, dig the eggs out of their mound of muck. Some hatchlings will bust out of their
shells using special egg teeth. This sharp bit of skin isn't a real tooth. It's a piece of
skin on a hatchling's snout that can slice through the shell's leathery inside layer. Your
baby can crack the hard outer layer by pushing its snout against it. Some of your
hatchlings will need help getting out. To break their shells, gently roll them between
your tongue and the roof of your mouth. Not too hard!

The hatchlings can make their own way to the water, but it's safer if you help them. Carry about ten in your mouth at a time, forming a cradle with your tongue.

Note to gharials: Your snout is too narrow and your teeth too sharp to carry your babies. Your nest hole may be on a beach that slopes into the water. In that case, your babies will glide down the sand as if on a slide! If the hole is farther away, lead your hatchlings to the water like a mother duck. (A really tough mother duck.)

17

Q. What will my babies
do all day?

A. They'll swim! Mothers usually keep an eye on them, though
babies in some species go it alone. Assuming, you're a claws-on
mommy (or daddy), every day will be family day at the swamp.
Your hatchlings will stay close together in a group called a pod.
Sometimes, you'll swim with them. Other times, you'll leave them in a
grassy part of the water while you hunt. You'll listen carefully, though.
If a baby is attacked by a predator, it will cry out. Then you'll rush
over to help. You'll roar at the predator, as if asking: "How would you
feel if somebody tried to eat you?" And then you'll eat it.

Unfortunately, some animals will get to your babies before you can. Fish will sneak up underwater. Birds will swoop down from above. Do your best, though, and a couple members of the pod will survive.

If you're a South American caiman, a foster mom might raise your hatchlings. The hatchlings grow up during the dry season. Without rain, the marsh where you live shrinks. Food is hard to find. To the other adult caimans, your hatchlings look a lot like dinner. So one night, you and your babies escape! Follow your instincts to the nearest swamp.

If another mama caiman is already there, you won't be able to stay. Grown-ups don't like having "swamp mates." But you can leave your babies with this mother. She won't eat them. In fact, your hatchlings might share their new home with many babies from other pods. It's like having one hundred brothers and sisters!

Q. What will my babies eat?

A. Nothing at first. Their bellies are still full from all that egg yolk. They'll get hungry in a few days or weeks. Don't expect them to eat wildcats, oxen, or even otters right away. Even though they have sharp teeth, they have little mouths! Small fish, snails, and insects are just right.

Once in a while, you'll feed your babies. You can let them tug at a chunk of meat hanging out of your mouth. They might even crawl in your mouth to look for leftovers! Usually they'll hunt their own food in the shallows of the swamp—or even on land. They'll do their hunting at night, just like you do. Crocodilians are, after all, nocturnal. When the sun rises, you'll all rest together.

Q. Where will the hatchlings sleep?

A. They'll sleep in the grass, on a lily pad, or even on you! While they bask on your head or back, you'll sleep with your mouth open, teeth shining in the sun. This cools you (like a panting dog!). It also warns other animals: "I'm sorry, I can't eat you right now. But if you mess with me or my babies and need to be eaten immediately, my teeth would be happy to assist you."

You and your babies bask to warm up. And you wallow to cool yourselves. That's because you're cold-blooded. This doesn't mean that your blood is always cold. Sometimes it's cold, sometimes it's hot, and sometimes it's in-between. Your body temperature depends on the temperature around you. Sunlight warms you. Mud and water cool you. Don't let your body get too cold. Then you won't have the energy to move. And you won't be able to protect your babies. But don't overheat, either. Try to stay just right. Be "just right" blooded!

Q. What happens next?

A. Your hatchlings will grow. American alligators, your newborns are 8 inches (20 centimeters) long. By the time the babies are one year old, they'll be 24 inches (60 cm) long. After that, they'll grow about 12 inches (30 cm) every year. At the age of two, they're far from full-grown. But it's time to kick them out of the swamp. You'll be ready to lay a new clutch of eggs. If your older children stick around, they might bother the new babies. And by "bother," I mean, "eat them."

Say, "See you later, alligator." Don't feel guilty, mama gator. American crocodiles leave home after just a few days! The youngsters will learn to survive. And as they get bigger, other animals will learn not to mess with them!

Male American alligators grow to be about 13 feet (4 m) long. Females are closer to 10 feet (3 m) long. Nile crocodiles, your boy babies will grow to be about 15 feet (4.6 m) long and your girls, 10 feet. Australian saltwater crocodiles, your grown boys could be 20 feet (6 m) long and weigh more than 1 ton (0.9 metric tons). When your babies are all grown up, they'll have no predators—except humans, that is.

Q. Will I really see my alligators "later"
(or my crocodiles "after a while")?

A. Possibly. Nile crocodiles, you live in a group. As your juveniles grow, they might join you. Sometimes, you'll even work together to take down a zebra or a wildebeest. If you're a daddy, you might be the dominant male in the group. Your children and the other youngsters will let you eat first—one of the more beautiful aspects of fatherhood.

However, most alligators and crocodiles prefer to be alone. Mamas, you'd think you would miss the hatchlings you guarded so closely. But for you, parting is natural. You've done your job. You raised many helpless babies to become a few strong crocodilians.

Soon they'll be guarding eggs of their own. They'll dream of babies who are big and tough. And their babies will be . . . someday. Until then, their mommy and daddy will take care of them . . . and any creature who messes with them too! Just like you did. Just like your parents did. Just like crocodilians have done for millions of years.

The End . . . and the Beginning.

GLOSSARY

alligator: a type of crocodilian known for its wide snout and rugged good looks. There are two types of alligators: the American alligator and the Chinese alligator. Alligator snouts are wider than crocodile snouts.

bask: to relax in the sun. Crocodiles must bask to warm their bodies because they are cold-blooded.

bayou: a slow-moving wetland river in the southern United States; to American alligators, paradise

caiman: a type of crocodilian that, along with alligators, is in the Alligatoridae family. There are six types of caimans, and all live in Central or South America. They look similar to alligators but tend to be smaller—4 to 12 feet (1.2 to 3.7 m) long.

clutch: a group of eggs in a nest

cold-blooded: an animal with a body temperature that is similar to the temperature of its surroundings

crocodile: a type of crocodilian known for its pointy snout and snazzy snaggleteeth. Unlike alligators, crocodiles' bottom teeth show when their mouths are closed. There are fourteen types of crocodiles.

dominant: having control over others; in the case of animals, having control over other members of the group or being capable of fighting off, outcompeting, or eating animals in other species

egg tooth: a piece of skin on a hatchling's snout that allows it to slice through the leathery inner layer of the eggshell

estuary: the area of water where a river meets the ocean

gharial: a type of crocodilian that has a long, narrow snout and eats fish. The only member of the family Gavialidae, it is also known as a gavial.

hatchling: a baby crocodilian that has hatched

instincts: built-in knowledge or behaviors

juvenile: a young crocodilian. The term *juvenile* usually refers to an animal that is older than a hatchling.

lagoon: a small body of water either connected to or near the ocean

mangrove swamp: a saltwater swamp in which trees and shrubs grow

marsh: a wetland in which grasses and small shrubs grow

mugger: a type of crocodile that lives in the rivers, lakes, and marshes of India and nearby countries. It has a wider snout than most crocodiles.

nest: a structure animals build to lay their eggs in. Crocodilian nests are made from leaves, grass, and mud or are dug as holes.

Nile: a river located in Africa that is the world's longest; to man-eating crocodiles, home sweet home

nocturnal: active at night

pod: a group of crocodilian hatchlings

predator: an animal that hunts and eats other animals

swamp: a still body of water in which trees and brush grow. Swamps can be freshwater or salt water.

wallow: to lie in the mud; also, a muddy area that fills with water

FURTHER READING AND WEBSITES

BOOKS

Arnosky, Jim. *Crocodile Safari*. New York: Scholastic Press, 2009.
Join the author on a canoe ride through the Florida Everglades to learn about the North American crocodile.

Dollar, Sam. *Caimans*. Austin, TX: Steadwell Books, 2001.
Discover more about caimans living in South and Central America through this book's simple yet informative text and photographs.

London, Jonathon. *Crocodile: Disappearing Dragon*. Cambridge, MA: Candlewick, 2001.
This illustrated book follows the yearly cycle of a female crocodile and looks at threats to American crocodiles.

Marcellino, Fred. *I, Crocodile*. New York: HarperCollins, 1999.
This is the funny fictional story of a crocodile uprooted from his home along the Nile and taken to Napoleon's court in Paris.

Pringle, Laurence. *Alligators and Crocodiles!: Strange and Wonderful*. Honesdale, PA: Boyds Mills Press, 2009.
This book introduces readers to twenty-one crocodilian species.

Silverman, Buffy. *Can You Tell an Alligator from a Crocodile?* Minneapolis: Lerner Publications Company, 2012.
Photos and text explain all about the differences between alligators and crocodiles.

LERNER
SOURCE

Expand learning beyond the printed book. Download free, complementary educational resources for this book from our website, www.lerneresource.com.

WEBSITES

Australian Animals
http://www.australianfauna.com
This site provides information about animals from Australia, including multiple crocodile species.

Crocodile Specialist Group
http://iucncsg.org/ph1/modules/Crocodilians/
This international organization is dedicated to conserving the twenty-three living species of crocodilians worldwide.

Crocodilians: Natural History and Conservation
http://www.crocodilian.com
This website features photos, videos, and detailed information about crocodilians from around the world.

Gharial Conservation Alliance
http://www.gharialconservation.org
This organization's website focuses on the conservation efforts to preserve gharials, a species of crocodilian native to India and Nepal.

Living Among Alligators
http://www.crocodopolis.net/lwa_safety.htm
This site provides information about how humans and alligators can safely live near each other.

St. Augustine Alligator Farm
http://www.alligatorfarm.us/videos/
These videos from the St. Augustine Alligator Farm in Florida offer a glimpse at the daily actions of alligators.

ABOUT THE AUTHOR

Bridget Heos is also the author of *What to Expect When You're Expecting Joeys: A Guide for Marsupial Parents (and Curious Kids)* and *What to Expect When You're Expecting Larvae: A Guide for Insect Parents (and Curious Kids)*. She has written more than twenty children's books and teaches creative writing to seventh and eighth gators. One of her favorite books growing up was *Lyle, Lyle, Crocodile*. She lives in Kansas City, Missouri, with her husband and three sons. You can visit her at www.authorbridgetheos.com.

ABOUT THE ILLUSTRATOR

Stéphane Jorisch is a full-time illustrator who has received several prestigious Canadian honors for his work, including a 1993 Governor General's Award; nominations for Governor General's Awards in 1995, 1997, and 1998; and nominations for the 1997 and 1999 Mr. Christie Book Awards. Jorisch works in a huge loft in Montreal, Quebec, with several other designers and illustrators. He believes that curiosity and a keen sense of observation are most important for an aspiring writer or artist.